W9-AEZ-033

REMBRANDT

BY MARC LE BOT

BONFINI PRESS

Title page: SELF-PORTRAIT, ca 1668
Oil on canvas, 38⅜″ × 25⁹⁄₁₆″ (82.5 × 65 cm)
Wallraf-Richartz Museum, Cologne

Series published under the direction of:
MADELEINE LEDIVELEC-GLOECKNER

Translated from the French:
MARIE-HÉLÈNE AGÜEROS

PRINTED IN ITALY – INDUSTRIE GRAFICHE CATTANEO S.P.A., BERGAMO
© 1990 BONFINI PRESS ESTABLISHMENT, VADUZ, LIECHTENSTEIN
ALL RIGHTS RESERVED. NO PART OF THIS BOOK MAY BE REPRODUCED OR UTILIZED IN ANY FORM OR BY ANY MEANS,
ELECTRONIC OR MECHANICAL, INCLUDING PHOTOCOPYING, RECORDING, OR ANY INFORMATION STORAGE AND RETRIEVAL SYSTEM,
WITHOUT PERMISSION IN WRITING FROM THE PUBLISHER

ARTIST IN HIS STUDIO, ca 1629
Oil in panel, 9¾″ × 12¼″ (24.8 × 31.7 cm)
Museum of Fine Arts, Boston
The Zoe Oliver Sherman Collection
Given in memory of Lillie Oliver Poor

Rembrandt's art is above all an art of light. But what is light, how do we experience it? Light is an uncertain reality; our eyes do not perceive it like an object or a unique phenomenon which could be easily outlined. Light is the essence of seeing, it is that which makes everything visible, and it contains every manner of seeing. Light is an event that is always about to happen. Consequently, it has fostered many intellectual systems by which man tried to think about light and the world made visible. Like all intellectual interpretations,

Artist Drawing from a Model, ca 1639
Pen and bistre, wash
7¼″ × 6⁵⁄₁₆″ (18.5 × 16 cm)
The British Museum, London

these systems vary according to place, time, and culture, and these transformations can best be traced through the history of painting rather than science. Along with line and color, Western cultures have used light to shape within an imaginary space that which Paul Cézanne called "the jumbled sensations we bring at birth." The notion of light that generally prevails today is still one that was formed during the Renaissance, while modern Western artists view that notion as only one among the many that are available to them. This classical notion of light is related to the actual visual experience, but it is a fairly recent notion and has remained dominant for no more than five or six centuries. We see it come about as an absolute rule of pictorial representation, take various forms, and soon disappear.

Rembrandt, who lived from 1606 to 1669, may have brought about the last creative period in the history of light and shapes during the Renaissance. A few other artists had played a similarly significant role before him: first Giotto (1266-1337), then Masaccio (1401-1428), Leonardo da Vinci (1452-1519), Titian (1488-1576) and the great Venetian painters, and finally Caravaggio (1570-1610). After Rembrandt, there were to be no more changes that would alter the structure of a painting, although there were some dazzling variations in the molding of shapes by light. Hence, Rembrandt's paintings appear as the final accomplishment of all the possibilities contained in the classical concept of light. Impressionism was to destroy this concept and reshuffle all the components in the study of light, but this reshuffling was to produce a very different approach to art.

Going back through our Western tradition, the representation of light was present in painting for several centuries before it was first recorded by Quintilianus, who lived from 30 A.D. to 100 A.D. According to Quintilianus, light was first depicted by the Greek painter Zeuxis, who lived in the fifth century B.C. and used contrasting dark and light tones, the play of light and shade, to shape objects and bodies and create a realistic rendering of volume and texture. No artist, however, from the Greek and Roman antiquity saw light as a link between the components of a painting. The Renaissance conceived of light as an atmosphere pervading the whole composition and defining each component's place in the space of the painting. Before the Renaissance,

The Artist's Studio, ca 1655-1656
Pen and ink, wash, touched with white body-color
(partly oxidized), 7⅞" × 7⁷⁄₁₆" (20 × 18.9 cm)
The Ashmoleum Museum, Oxford

7

Row of Trees in an Open Field
ca 1636
Pen, bistre, and wash
5¹¹⁄₁₆″ × 9⁹⁄₁₆″ (12.8 × 24.4 cm)
Akademie der Bildenden Künste
Kupferstichkabinett, Vienna

artists depicted separate three-dimensional shapes, each lit separately, rather than a whole composition held together by a unifying light. Paintings from the antiquity created fragmented views, mostly of mythical themes that did not need to follow a strict chronology. Light was used in a similar manner throughout the Middle Ages, but medieval artists were mostly preoccupied with the respective symbolic value of different colors.

When painters discovered linear perspective, they also used a single source of light, creating an "atmospheric perspective" that gave their painting its orientation by crossing its whole space. Both perspectives were equally necessary for a unified view of a space. In the fifteenth century, when the representation of geometric perspective had made decisive progress, most artists had to resolve the following problem: When the same red tone is used for both distant and close objects, the effect of distance is canceled. There is no depth of perspective and the space of the painting becomes vertical. Then came Leonardo da Vinci, who reconciled the perspective depicted through lines and that depicted through colors hit by light. After him, artists explicitly used two different optical illusions, both related to the visual experience of distance. Distant colors turn progressively blue and gray, just as parallel lines seem to touch one another at the point of infinity. Thus man's everyday experience became the painter's true vision. The works and debates of the time, however, showed the fragility of this approach based on chiaroscuro. Opinions could differ greatly and much was at stake: If the reality of the visible world was not one, if perception of lines and colors referred to hardly

A Winter Landscape, 1648-1652
Pen, brush, and brown ink on cream paper
2⅝″ × 6¼″ (6.8 × 16 cm)
The Fogg Art Museum, Cambridge
Massachusetts
Bequest of Charles A. Loeser

compatible explanations and experiences, then the fundamental beliefs of classical humanism were threatened. This is where Rembrandt's work becomes so significant. Its light and shade are both interdependent and clashing violently. He created a visual space where the notion of close and far distance tends to disappear. And one may wonder whether this treatment of chiaroscuro does not express a terrible anxiety, the doubts of an artist who realized that man's destiny might not lead him to the concept of one world secured by concepts of God as One and Man as an individual. His art may reflect the pain of every man as he faces his fate with a divided mind and uncertain references.

What was the situation of artists when Rembrandt started to paint? In what circumstances did they perceive the main artistic debates of their time? The Netherlands won their freedom from Spanish domination in 1609, three years after Rembrandt was born. The new nation's existence was based on trade. It was ruled by bourgeois

The Three Trees, 1643
Etching, only state
8⁵⁄₁₆″ × 11″
(21.1 × 28 cm)
Kunsthalle, Hamburg
Photo Elke Walford

The Angler, 1654-1655
Pen and bistre
4¹⁵⁄₁₆″ × 6¾″
(12.6 × 17.2 cm)
Statens Konstmuseer
Stockholm

merchants, and the structure of its state was quite different from that of the rest of Europe, ruled by kings and princes. Culture, however, was common to all Europe, and it was an essential component of all forms of power. Most of the time, the churches, princes, and bourgeois became aware of the values supporting their power only after these values were heralded in cultural works, especially paintings commissioned for prestige. In Holland, however, pictures played also a unique role. Paintings were more in demand than anywhere else and this demand was different. More people held a share of power in a bourgeois state than in a monarchy; any man with sufficient wealth could take part in the exercise of a power based on economic success. As a result, Dutch artists did not only paint for palaces and churches. Any house could have paintings on its walls. Although the meaning of life remained tied to religious beliefs, it was also rooted, more than in any other country, in daily work, pleasures, and simple rituals. Dutch painters also enjoyed a special status. At the beginning of the fifteenth century, at the time of the first Renaissance, Italian artists were viewed as intellectuals; many were theoreticians of art, who were close to scientists and philosophers. Nothing of the sort happened in Holland, where artists remained craftsmen. Their material circumstances were often modest, even when their production was large. It is therefore the more interesting to understand why Rembrandt should have been so ambitious socially, and how he achieved both fame and wealth, although he was to go bankrupt at the end of his life.

Two negative factors could have played against the arts. Catholicism had been swept aside by the Protestant faith, in which an iconoclastic movement advocated against pictures on religious themes. In spite of this statement of principles, the new faith in Holland was very tolerant toward its many sects and their wide range of opinions on the subject of art. Deep-rooted religious feelings prevented too strong an opposition

A Foot Operation, ca 1628
Pen and bistre, brush, brown wash
and gray India ink, 12⁷⁄₁₆″ × 10⁷⁄₁₆″ (31.7 × 26.6 cm)
Galleria degli Uffizi
Gabinetti dei Disegni e Stampe, Florence
Photo Nicolò Orsi Battaglini, Florence

The Naughty Boy, ca 1635
Pen and bistre, wash, white body-color
some black chalk, 8⅛″ × 5⅝″ (20.6 × 14.3 cm)
Staatliche Museen, Preußischer Kulturbesitz
Kupferstichkabinett, Berlin-Dahlem
Photo Jörg P. Anders, Berlin

11

Portrait of an Old Man
Rembrandt's Father, ca 1630
Red and black chalk, wash in bistre
7⁷/₁₆" × 9⁷/₁₆" (18.9 × 24 cm)
The Ashmoleum Museum, Oxford

against the production of pictures inspired by religious beliefs. Moreover, fewer works were commissioned by the aristocracy. The ruling bourgeoisie largely replaced the church and aristocracy as a source of commissions, and it was interested mostly in a formal representation of the actual life of the community. This preference for themes drawn from daily life came with new artistic movements, among which Rembrandt's art of light was most revealing.

In 1640, at the height of Rembrandt's fame, an Englishman named Peter Mundy published a book of his travels. He had lived for a while in Holland, and he wrote that nobody could outdo the Dutch in their art of painting and their taste for pictures, and that the country counted a great number of excellent artists, among whom he named Rembrandt.[1] He noted that everybody tried to decorate their houses with priceless works, particularly the room in the front or on the street. Butchers and bakers were in no way inferior to other tradesmen in that regard, and paintings were prominently displayed in their shops. The works of Rembrandt mentioned by Mundy as an example were not meant to decorate only private houses and shops. But many were. This was certainly a factor in the artist's considerable production, and it fostered a great number of paintings, drawings, and prints, the quality of which equaled that of his greatest pictures. Many works formerly believed to be Rembrandt's are now questioned; he was often imitated by contemporaries, and he sometimes touched up and signed his students' paintings, which would then fetch a higher price. In spite of these restrictions, it is estimated that he produced six hundred paintings, fourteen hundred drawings, and three hundred etchings.

Rembrandt was fifteen when he started as an apprentice in the studio of Jakob van Swanenburgh, in Leyden. The city had then fifty thousand inhabitants, its size and trade second only to Amsterdam's. It was a lively cultural center, with a famous

(1) *The Travels of Peter Mundy in Europe and Asia: 1608-1667*, vol. IV. London, 1925.

THE CLEMENCY OF TITUS
UNIDENTIFIED HISTORY PAINTING, 1626
Oil on panel, 25⁵⁄₁₆″ × 47⅝″
(89.8 × 121 cm)
Stedelijk Museum de Lakenhal, Leyden

13

ANDROMEDA CHAINED TO A ROCK, 1627-1628
Oil on panel
13⁹⁄₁₆″ × 9¹³⁄₁₆″ (34.5 × 25 cm)
Mauritshuis, The Hague

THE ABDUCTION OF PROSERPINA, ca 1632
Oil on panel, 33¼″ × 31¼″ (84.5 × 79.3 cm)
Staatliche Museen, Preußischer Kulturbesitz
Gemäldegalerie, Berlin-Dahlem

Diana and Actaeon, ca 1662-1665
Pen and bistre, wash, white body-color
9⅝" × 13⅝"
(24.6 × 34.7 cm)
Staatliche Kunstsammlungen, Kupferstichkabinett
Dresden

university that attracted, among others, the French philosopher René Descartes. Rembrandt Harmenszoon van Rijn (Rembrandt, son of Harmen of the Rhine) was the eighth in a family of nine children. His father was a well-to-do miller, whose name indicates that his mill stood on the river that crossed the city. Young Rembrandt received a very good education. Until 1620 he attended Leyden's Latin school, where the teaching was based on the study of Latin literature and done in Latin. After Rembrandt died, the inventory of his library showed that, aside from the Bible, he owned books by Ovid, Tacit, Livy, as well as the "History of the Jews" by Flavius Josephus. His interest in the Jews stemmed from his religion and reading from the Bible, as well as the fact that his house in Amsterdam stood near the Jewish quarters, where he could observe remarkable faces and characters. In 1620, Rembrandt enrolled at the university in Leyden. He left after three months to devote himself to painting. He had received, however, a thorough grounding in the liberal arts and an education founded on the knowledge of Greek and Roman history and mythology. Aside from the Bible and the observation of his contemporaries' daily life, this is where he was to find the themes for his paintings. In those days, a Dutch artist rarely enjoyed such a high education.

What did Rembrandt learn from his first teacher, Jakob van Swanenburgh?[1] He aspired to become a "history painter," as history painting was viewed as the most elevated genre during the Renaissance. The prestige of such a genre indicates that artists were achieving at the time the status of intellectuals, although this was less true in Holland than in Italy or even France. History painting presented great biblical and mythological stories, the moral and religious meaning of which was taught at school. It also presented significant events related to the political development of modern society. In other words, such paintings were to make explicit the meaning that society saw in its own history as well as the meaning that each citizen, in this context, could give to his personal destiny. In 1624, this first lesson learned from Jakob van Swanenburgh was strengthened when Rembrandt stayed in Amsterdam for six months and worked under

(1) Born in Leyden in 1571, Jakob van Swanenburgh went to Italy and worked in Venice and Naples. He returned to Leyden in 1617, where he died in 1638.

Tobias Accusing Anna of Stealing the Kid, 1626
Oil on panel, 15¹³⁄₁₆″ × 11¾″ (40.1 × 29.9 cm). Rijksmuseum, Amsterdam

JOSEPH ACCUSED BY POTIPHAR'S WIFE, 1655
Oil on canvas, 44¹¹⁄₁₆″ × 35⅜″ (113,5 × 90 cm)
Staatliche Museen, Preußischer Kulturbesitz
Gemäldegalerie, Berlin-Dahlem

TOBIT AND HIS WIFE, 1659
Oil on panel, 15¹⁵⁄₁₆″ × 21³⁄₁₆″ (40.5 × 54 cm)
Museum Boymans-van Beuningen, Rotterdam
Willem van der Vorm Foundation

a prestigious master, Pieter Lastman.[1] Lastman had been to Italy, where he had seen the works of Caravaggio and Adam Elsheimer.[2] His history paintings belong to the Dutch tradition, but he succeeded in avoiding some fashionable clichés. His figures each have a personality expressed in gestures and features. However, the dramatic tension and realistic details of his paintings were weakened by a certain blandness in the composition. Rembrandt was very impressed by Lastman's work, in which he often found a direct inspiration, although the strong effects of light in his own work made it also very different. Most importantly, Lastman's teaching made him familiar with the contemporary issue of the treatment of light in painting, which was brilliantly developed by followers of Caravaggio.

Rembrandt returned to Leyden in 1625. He was only nineteen years old and he opened his own studio. Such precociousness was possible at the time because young people went through a very thorough apprenticeship in the studios of masters. It was made easier for Rembrandt in particular because there were no painters' guilds in Leyden, which could have imposed a time frame on beginners. The first known painting by Rembrandt is *The Martyrdom of St. Stephen*, dated 1625 (see page 21). It shows what Rembrandt had learned from his masters and chosen to retain from their teaching. The theme of *The Martyrdom of St. Stephen* is taken from the Lives of the Saints, which

(1) Born in Amsterdam in 1583, Pieter Lastman left for Italy around 1604. At the beginning of 1607, he returned to Amsterdam, where his work was highly regarded. Until 1606 he painted scenes from the Bible and landscapes from the antiquity in the style of Elsheimer. After 1620, his paintings showed the influence of Caravaggio's powerful style. He died in Amsterdam in 1633.

(2) Born in Frankfurt in 1574, Adam Elsheimer was known for his history and landscape paintings, as well as his etchings. He left Germany when he was very young, settled in Rome around 1600, after a stay in Venice, and died there in 1610 or 1620. He continued to paint in a very detailed German tradition and was most interested in highly contrasting effects of light.

The Vision of Daniel (Daniel and the Angel Gabriel by the River Ulai)
ca 1652
Reed-pen and wash in bistre and white body-color
6½″ × 9⁹⁄₁₆″ (16.5 × 24.3 cm)
Musée du Louvre, Paris
Cabinet des Dessins. Legs L. Bonnat
Photo Réunion des Musées Nationaux
Paris

THE MARTYRDOM OF ST. STEPHEN, 1625
Oil on panel, 35³⁄₁₆″ × 48¹¹⁄₁₆″ (89.5 × 123.6 cm)
Musée des Beaux-Arts, Lyons
Photo Studio Basset, Lyons

the Christian religion used as an example to help understand man's destiny. Among all the themes offered to history painters, Rembrandt had first chosen an execution after torture, one of the many indications in his work of his real fascination for scenes of violence. The drama of Stephen's martyrdom is heightened by the composition of the painting. The executioners form a group whose features and posture express a cruelty contrasting with the posture and features of the saint praying. On the right- and left-hand sides, Rembrandt painted a group of horsemen and a cityscape. The static effect and darker colors of these two parts stress the brightly lit intensity at the center of the composition. The slightly acid colors evoke the Mannerist style of Pieter Lastman. Most striking is the contrast between the luminous colors at the center and the darkened tones on the sides of the composition. It is close to the manner in which Caravaggio and his many followers painted light. Rembrandt was soon to treat this contrast between light and shade in a manner as innovative as Caravaggio's. More than through his choice of themes, it was through the contrast between light and shade that Rembrandt was to express best the intensity, and sometimes violence, of human relationships.

This treatment of light was one of the artistic innovations that were to mark the sixteenth and seventeenth centuries. Caravaggio's light was not meant to hold together the components of a composition. It cut through the space of a painting and created a sharp contrast between light and dark areas. In *The Martyrdom of St. Stephen*, Rembrandt also used a stream of light, which falls on the center of the composition from a source above and slightly to the side of the painting. We may find that it creates a rather theatrical effect, like a spotlight on actors on a stage. Rembrandt's contemporaries viewed it as a metaphor, a ray of sunlight through the clouds, a symbol of God's awareness of Man's tragic life. Artists like the Le Nain brothers, Georges de La Tour, and Rembrandt drew a parallel between this effect and the artificial light of lamps. A painting dated around 1629, *Christ at Emmaus*, underscores the artificial aspect of such composition. Two figures are depicted against the light and seem to mirror one another: Christ in the front, and a servant woman in the back of the room, where people are eating (see page 64). Caravaggio did not feel the need to support the staging of a painting with such tangible reality as the light of a candle or an oil lamp. Similarly, Rembrandt's extreme effects of light could not be justified by the observation of reality. Light in Rembrandt's paintings — in a manner different from Caravaggio's — became a matter of pure painting. It was purely pictorial, without any reference to daily visual experience. The painting expressed the artist's thoughts and the viewer was provoked into thinking by visual devices that referred only to painting itself.

These extreme plays of light in both Caravaggio's and Rembrandt's works were part of a history in which they find their meaning. The history of the art of painting shows the artist continually questioning the effects he produces. Leonardo da Vinci's role was decisive in the reconciliation of linear and color perspectives, which had been incompatible since Giotto. He used the chiaroscuro, the sfumato or shading of figures

THE BAPTISM OF THE EUNUCH, 1626.   Oil on panel, 25⅛″ × 18¹¹⁄₁₆″ (64 × 47.5 cm)
Stichting Het Catharijnenconvent Ruben de Heer, Utrecht

and objects to insure an imperceptible passage from one color to another. The Venetian painters were just as imaginative in their quest for unity of vision, using half tones to create a seamless continuity in the space of a painting. Caravaggio's art created havoc, causing Nicolas Poussin to remark later, "This man had come to destroy painting." [1] Before him, painters had depicted the gradual passage from light to shade. Caravaggio used light as a sharp tool to carve out that which had captured the painter's attention. Leonardo da Vinci had conceived of light as a third element which reconciled lines and colors, while Caravaggio used light to break up that which is visible and cause its components to clash. Rembrandt's light is of a different nature, and it stems from a different view of the human drama, but his art played also on the register of intensity, even violence.

The Conspiracy of Claudius Civilis, 1660-1661
Pen and bistre, wash, some white body-color
4³/₁₆″ × 7¹/₁₆″ (10.6 × 18 cm)
Staatliche Graphische Sammlung, Munich

The following year, in 1626, Rembrandt painted *The Baptism of the Eunuch*, in which light cut more sharply through the canvas (see page 23). It also featured another trait typical of his work, at least in the first part of his life: Rembrandt had a taste for the strange and unusual, for costumes, and even exoticism. His art was always meant to startle the viewer, either with sharp effects of light, or strange scenes, settings, and clothes. The painter's eye was supposed to be full of wonders, perceiving the unexpected in that which was familiar and combining the pleasure of seeing with a feeling of disturbing strangeness. Rembrandt used every technique to express this fundamental approach to art. Although he never left Leyden to go any farther than Amsterdam and Utrecht, and his whole life was spent in a sixty-mile radius from his birthplace, he, more than any other artist of his time, was captivated by things originating from elsewhere. Holland was then a portal for trade with the East. When Rembrandt settled in Amsterdam in 1631, he first lived in the house of an art and curio dealer, Hendrick van Uylenburgh. By the time he married Van Uylenburgh's niece, Saskia, he had invested the considerable sum of a thousand guilders in the business of this man, at whose house he could see objects that came from all over the world. But Leyden may have already given him an opportunity for unusual encounters. The city was quite cosmopolitan because of trade but also because its

---

(1) Born in 1594 in Villers, Nicolas Poussin decided to devote himself to painting in 1612. He left for Paris, and in 1624 fulfilled his dream to go to Italy. He first went to Venice, where he studied Titian's works, then to Rome, where he stayed until he died in 1665, with a brief stay in Paris from 1640 to 1642. Regarded as a master of French painting, he admired mostly the paintings of Raphael, and detested those of Caravaggio. He believed in a very rational approach to art and after 1642 gave gradually more importance to landscape painting.

THE CONSPIRACY OF CLAUDIUS CIVILIS:
THE OATH, 1661-1662
Oil on canvas, 77⅛″ × 121⅝″ (196 × 309 cm)
Statens Konstmuseer, Stockholm

Self-Portrait as a Beggar, 1630
Etching, 4⁵⁄₁₆″ × 2¹¹⁄₁₆″ (11 × 6.9 cm)
Kunsthalle, Hamburg
Photo Elke Walford, Hamburg

university attracted foreigners. He could see in the streets students from distant countries, dressed in traditional national clothes. His pictures often featured such objects and ornaments, without any reason of verisimilitude. Rembrandt's taste for exoticism was merely another means to depict intense human relationships: The effects of light and strange objects both expressed a sharp sense of otherness.

The Baptism of the Eunuch was among his first works to show both approaches. The theme of the painting was drawn from the Acts of the Apostles: Philip christens a Moorish eunuch. Clothing, headgear, furs, and embroideries take the viewer's imagination far from Europe and Dutch landscapes. Within one year Rembrandt had stopped using flat and acid colors in the manner of Pieter Lastman. He used quick, short brush strokes and thick paints. Although the protective layers of varnish that have been applied on the painting through the years have darkened its colors and given it a reddish sheen, the contrasting tones of gold, red, and blue are visually very effective: Using a musical metaphor, they could be described as deep because they use the three primary colors that are now regarded as the source of all other colors.

An effect of strangeness due to the choice of themes and ornaments, sharply contrasting light, a quick brush stroke, and thick paints were to be fairly constant features of Rembrandt's work. His last large canvas, the last history painting he created for an official building, was finished in 1662, seven years before he died. Although *The Conspiracy of Claudius Civilis: The Oath* has since been partially destroyed, it is still a striking arrangement of red and gold tones (see page 25). Parts of the picture are strongly illuminated by the light at the center, the source of which the viewer cannot see; others stand against that light. The brush stroke is rough. This painting in a "heroic" genre had been commissioned for the Town Hall in Amsterdam. The hero was Claudius Civilis, to whom the Batavi swore to fight the Roman invaders till they

SELF-PORTRAIT WITH TOUSLED HAIR, ca 1628
Oil on panel
8⅞″ × 7⅜″ (22.6 × 18.7 cm)
Rijskmuseum, Amsterdam

REMBRANDT'S MOTHER, ca 1628-1630
Oil on copper, 6⅛″ × 4¾″ (15.5 × 12.2 cm)
Salzburger Landessammlungen
Residenzgalerie, Salzburg

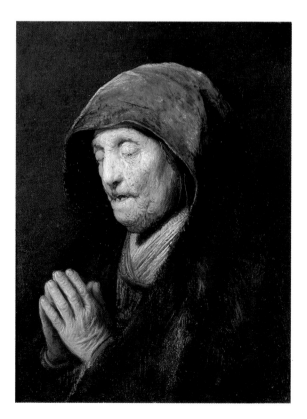

Rembrandt's Mother, 1628
Etching II/II, 2⁹⁄₁₆″ × 2½″ (6.5 × 6.3 cm)
Kunsthalle, Hamburg
Photo Elke Walford
Hamburg

died. The work was meant to extol the valor of the Dutch people, who had won their independence from Spain in 1609. The aldermen of Amsterdam rejected the painting, however, because it did not abide by conventional rules of heroic painting: It did not feature a grand staging, an impressive setting, and expressive gesturing. Rembrandt's work was made of a dramatic tension imparted by contrasting colored lights. Human drama attracted the artist's attention, rather than ceremonies and social rituals. His work was to turn away from the spectacular and toward the expression of an inner reflection and human relationships often characterized by secrecy, as is the case here.

Rembrandt in a Cap
Open-Mouthed and Staring, 1630
Etching I/II, 2″ × 1¹³⁄₁₆″ (5.1 × 4.6 cm)
Kunsthalle, Hamburg
Photo Elke Walford, Hamburg

Self-Portrait
Looking Over His Shoulder, 1630
Etching III/III, 2¹³⁄₁₆″ × 2⅜″ (7.2 × 6 cm)
Kunsthalle, Hamburg
Photo Elke Walford, Hamburg

THE MONEY-CHANGER, 1627
Oil on panel, 12⁷⁄₁₆″ × 16¹¹⁄₁₆″
(31.7 × 42.5 cm)
Staatliche Museen, Preußischer Kulturbesitz
Gemäldegalerie, Berlin-Dahlem

THE APOSTLE PAUL AT HIS DESK, ca 1629-1630.   Oil on panel, 18⁷⁄₁₆″ × 15⁵⁄₁₆″ (47 × 39 cm)
Germanisches Nationalmuseum, Nuremberg

JEREMIAH LAMENTING THE DESTRUCTION OF JERUSALEM, 1630
Oil on panel, 22¹⁵⁄₁₆″ × 18⁵⁄₁₆″ (58.3 × 46.6 cm). Rijksmuseum, Amsterdam

A Scholar in a Room with a Winding Stair, 1632
Oil on panel, 11″ × 13⅜″ (28 × 34 cm)
Musée du Louvre, Paris
Photo Réunion des Musées Nationaux, Paris

ARISTOTLE WITH A BUST OF HOMER, 1653
Oil on canvas, 56½″ × 53¾″ (143.5 × 136.5 cm)
The Metropolitan Museum of Art
New York

33

Christ with the Sick Around Him
Receiving Little Children
(The Hundred Guilder Print)
A Study, ca 1642-1645
Etching and drypoint I/VI
11⅛" × 15½" (28.3 × 39.5 cm)
Staatliche Museen
Preußischer Kulturbesitz
Kupferstichkabinett
Berlin-Dahlem

The features of the Batavi are barely visible: The viewer can only see the parts of their face that are struck by light. The figure sitting at the left of Claudius Civilis is painted almost in a flat tint, his features blurred, his face a golden splash outlined against a dark background. Between the 1620s and the years of Rembrandt's old age, his work expressed his many-faceted reflections on human destiny. What remained constant were his striking effects of light, his preference for the unusual, and his fascination with the exact moment when the drama comes to a head and unfolds.

In his youth, Rembrandt showed that he combined an awareness of the drama of life with a curious mind in the perpetual pursuit of that which, in the daily life, would surprise him and capture his eyes. The Bible also fired his imagination for the unusual. But, most striking of all, his own body and face were the first source of his daily wonder. By common standards, Rembrandt was an ugly man, and he knew it. From the very early work, he scrutinized himself and questioned his ugliness. He made himself even uglier by depicting himself as a beggar, or donning military or Middle-Eastern clothes. His *Self-Portrait with Tousled Hair* in Amsterdam (see page 27) and the *Self-Portrait* in Munich, dated both 1629, feature a young man raising his face in defiance. The *Self-Portraits* in the Isabelle Stewart Gardner Museum in Boston and the Mauritshuis in The Hague, also dated 1629, stare down at the viewer. Around the same time, Rembrandt made many sketches of the destitute encountered in the streets of Leyden, with whom he identified symbolically in his self-portrait as a beggar. He perceived the decay of body and mind as an expression of his tragic feeling of life, while the insolent defiance of some self-portraits testified for the artist's ability to confront every facet of reality, even the most frightening ones. As a consequence, the young man looks undauntedly, almost cruelly, at faces destroyed by old age. The portrait of his aging mother praying, painted in 1629, is among the harshest of these "realist" paintings, inasmuch as realism is attracted by the cruel sides of life (see page 27).

Old Man with a Book, 1628
Red and black chalk, heightened with white
11⅛″ × 8¼″ (29.5 × 21 cm)
Staatliche Museen, Preußischer Kulturbesitz
Kupferstichkabinett, Berlin-Dahlem
Photo Jörg P. Anders, Berlin

SIMEON'S SONG AND PRAISE. THE PRESENTATION OF JESUS IN THE TEMPLE, 1631
Oil on panel, 24″ × 18⅞″ (61 × 48 cm).   Mauritshuis, The Hague

CHRIST AND THE WOMAN TAKEN IN ADULTERY, 1644
Oil on panel, 32¹⁵⁄₁₆″ × 25¹¹⁄₁₆″ (83.8 × 65.4 cm)
National Gallery, London

ST. PETERS'S DENIAL, 1660
Oil on canvas, 60⁹⁄₁₆″ × 66½″ (154 × 169 cm)
Rijksmuseum, Amsterdam

CHRIST BEFORE PILATE AND THE PEOPLE, 1634
Oil on paper laid down on canvas, 21⅜″ × 17½″ (54.2 × 44.5 cm). National Gallery, London

Christ and His Disciples, 1634
Pen in brown, gray, and black wash
black, red, and green chalk heightened with white
14¹⁄₁₆″ × 18¹³⁄₁₆″ (35.7 × 47.8 cm)
Teylers Museum, Haarlem

Crist in the Storm of the Sea of Galilee, ca 1654-1655
Pen and bistre
7¾″ × 11¹³⁄₁₆″ (19.7 × 30 cm)
Staatliche Kunstsammlungen, Kupferstichkabinett
Dresden

The Good Samaritan Arriving at the Inn
ca 1641-1643
Pen and bistre, wash, some corrections with white
7¼″ × 11¼″ (18.4 × 28.7 cm)
The British Museum, London

The word *realism* is always difficult to use properly. It is used to describe certain aspects of Rembrandt's work and underline that he did not ignore the hardships and cruelties of life, in spite of his attraction for the noble staging of history painting. Unlike Pieter Lastman, he refused to idealize. He was not a proper realist, however: Although he did not paint idealized academic figures, his splendid effects of light added glory to everything, even the mediocre and the terrifying. *The Money-Changer* in the museum in Berlin is a genre scene, drawn from the daily life of merchants (see page 29). A bright light, the source of which is, once again, hidden in the center of the painting, seems to create an energy that strengthens the viewer's perception. Rembrandt may not have depicted his figures according to an ideal canon of beauty, in the manner in which Raphael was considered the master, but he extolled life. He viewed mankind as a body which, like that of his mother, ages and bears the mask of its death; he also viewed it as an active mind, which brought life to several portraits of philosophers that he painted around this time. *Aristotle with a Bust of Homer*, painted in 1653, may be the most significant of these imaginary portraits (see page 33). The bust of the old poet and the coat of the philosopher are painted in the same golden tone, which illuminates the picture. This unity of color may be a symbol for a unity of meditation,

A Man in Oriental Costume, 1633
Oil on panel
33¹¹⁄₁₆″ × 25¹⁄₁₆″ (85.8 × 63.8 cm)
Alte Pinakothek, Munich
Photo Joachim Blauel/Artothek, Peissenberg

Two Busts of Orientals in Turbans
ca 1633
Pen and bistre
7⅛″ × 5⅝″ (18.2 × 14.3 cm)
Musée Royaux des Beaux-Arts, Brussels

Portrait of Saskia in a Staw Hat, 1633
Silver point on white prepared vellum
7¼" × 4³⁄₁₆" (18.5 × 10.7 cm)
Staatliche Museen, Preußischer Kulturbesitz
Kupferstichkabinett, Berlin-Dahlem

which the artist's work projected in contemporary times. The theme of the thinker was already an obsession in Rembrandt's early work. *The Apostle Paul at His Desk* in Nuremberg is a "man of the book" (1629-1630, see page 30). And *A Scholar in a Room with a Winding Stair* in the Louvre, also dated 1629, is an extraordinary staging of Man's greatness and the life of the mind (see page 32). The figure of the philosopher fills a dark corner in the picture, but a bright light pours into this place of meditation from the stained-glass window. The artist glorifies intellectual work by placing the philosopher in a monumental setting, where light is a symbol for the mind illuminating life. This symbolism, here and everywhere in Rembrandt's work, points to the common achievement of masterpieces in painting: Great art is that which gives a symbolic meaning to its own formal devices, such as the chiaroscuro in this painting. The theme of the painting, or the story it depicts, is made greater by the very shapes and technique used to extol moral and intellectual values.

In his humanist belief in the strength of mind, Rembrandt would mix at times dreamlike elements and reality, in order for the latter to better reveal its secret greatness. He observed his surroundings and he transformed them. The talents he had shown in his early work developed after he settled in 1631 in Amsterdam, where his art could blossom more than in Leyden. His fame was already such that he received commissions from the wealthiest patrons in Holland, whose demand for quality was the greatest. That year he painted *The Presentation of Jesus in the Temple*, a picture the size of a small oil on panel but grandiose in its staging (see page 37). Light streams on the Christ Child, His Mother, and the priests greeting them. Blue, red, and gold are the dominant colors. This light, which must come from the high arches of the temple, leaves most of the place in semidarkness. The staging is striking: The majestic architectural setting evokes religious awe; but the figures of Joseph, Mary, and the elders bending over the child are everyday types such as Rembrandt could observe. Real life was thus tied to the dream of another world

SASKIA AS FLORA, 1634. Oil on canvas, 49³⁄₁₆″ × 39¹³⁄₁₆″ (125 × 101 cm)
Hermitage Museum, Leningrad. Photo Aurora Publishing, Leningrad

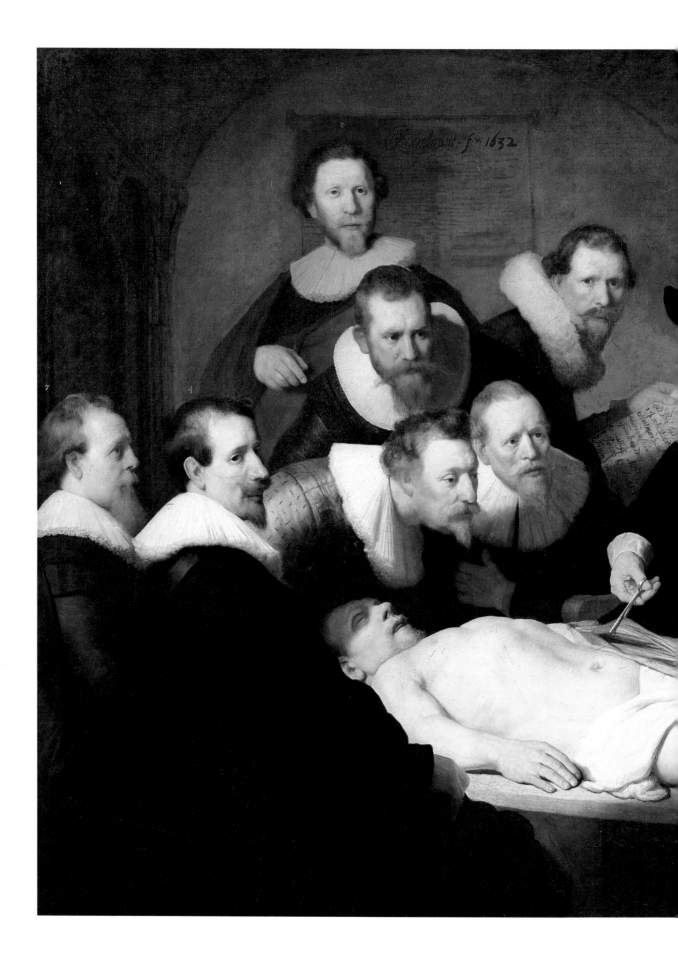

DOCTOR NICOLAES TULP DEMONSTRATING
THE ANATOMY OF THE ARM, 1632
Oil on canvas
66¹¹⁄₁₆″ × 85¼″ (169.5 × 216.5 cm)
Mauritshuis, The Hague

47

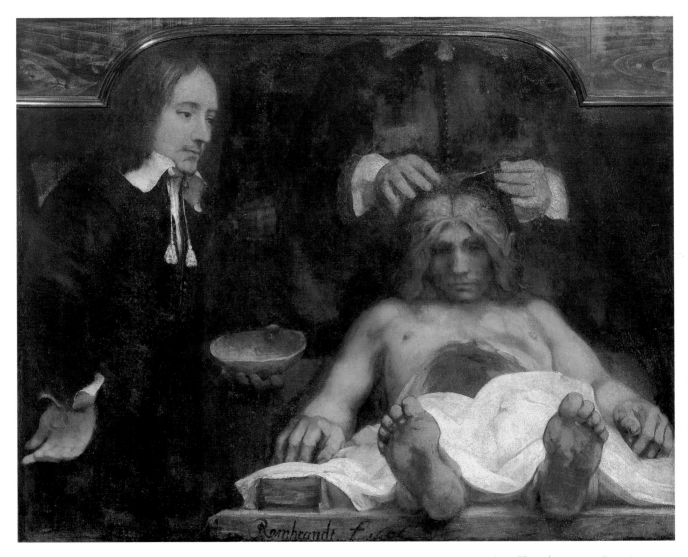

THE ANATOMY LESSON
OF DR. JOAN DEYMAN, 1656
Oil on canvas
39⅜″ × 52¾″ (100 × 134)
Rijksmuseum, Amsterdam

*Anatomy Lesson
of Dr. Joan Deyman, ca 1656
Pen drawing and bistre
4⁵⁄₁₆″ × 5³⁄₁₆″ (10.9 × 13.1 cm)
Rijksprintenkabinett, Amsterdam*

Boy Drawing at a Desk (probably Titus), 1655-1656
Pen and bistre and brush, rubbed with the finger
7³/₁₆" × 5⁷/₁₆" (18.2 × 13.9 cm)
Staatliche Kunstsammlungen
Kupferstichkabinett, Dresden

filled with glorious heavenly light. And this shining light was a symbol for the secret presence of God shaping Man's life. The technique itself was also meant to be the concrete expression of such thoughts, so as to be noticed by the viewer and lead him to his meditation: Here, a hard brush dug colored grooves; there, a soft brush stroked the texture of a fabric or the surface of the skin without leaving any trace.

Since the Renaissance, traditional themes offered to painters were meant to call upon the power of dreams. Rembrandt never ceased to paint the marvelous stories of the Bible and Greek mythology. And he always mixed the splendor of dreams with elements of sharp "realism." Thus the *Man in Oriental Costume*, painted in Amsterdam in 1633: The man's turban and coat are decorated with gold embroideries; his headgear features a plume and a string of pearls; but his face is swollen and worn by age (see page 43). The same mixture of dreamlike beauty and realism could be found in themes based on biblical or mythological stories. Many artists of the time used such themes to suggest moments of happiness in ancient times, either moments of truth — when they used stories from the Bible — or moments of ideal beauty — when they called on the Greek tradition, in which sculpture testified to such beauty. They maintained the theme of an original paradise or beauty subsequently lost. Rembrandt's approach was the opposite. He believed that truth and beauty are among us, here and now. When he painted legendary figures, he took the people around him as models, often his wife Saskia, or men and women he came across in the streets. In 1633 and 1634 respectively, he painted *Saskia with a Veil* (Rijksmuseum, Amsterdam) and *Saskia as Flora* (see page 45). Rembrandt was not dreaming of a nostalgic past as he was painting the portrait of his wife. He decked Saskia with jewels and precious fabrics; he made her into a queen or goddess; but this was to extol her actual presence at his side. There is an eroticism in these paintings that brings to mind Charles Baudelaire's words, when he wrote of the "sonorous jewels" adorning the body of his beloved. But the vision that the painter as a man has of the woman as a model reaches beyond the exaltation of his desire for her. When Rembrandt and other classical artists made pictures of mythological goddesses, such as

THE NIGHTWATCH, 1642
Oil on canvas
143½″ × 172⅟₁₆″ (363 × 437 cm)
Rijksmuseum, Amsterdam

the *Minerva* of 1635, they wished to give a tangible form to ethical qualities of mankind. Figures in paintings and characters in the theater of the time expressed in a spectacular fashion that which was at stake in human relations. And the spectacular presentation of female figures as Flora or Minerva, bringing forth the notions of fecundity and warlike instincts, evoked ancient paganism and its sacralization of daily life.

Rembrandt was painting many portraits at the time and each gave him another entry into the establishment. Artists had then a definite place and role in society. Romantics have wrongly viewed Rembrandt as the first doomed artist, based on the mistaken idea that he died poor. This is easy to understand. Artists had a marginal status in nineteenth-century industrial society. Painters, poets, and musicians experienced this marginality as a curse, which they imagined to have been the lot of artists of all times. And because artists may still be somewhat marginal today, the legend of Rembrandt as a doomed painter has survived. Reality was quite different. As early as the 1620s, and even more so after the 1630s, Rembrandt painted many portraits because he had become famous very quickly and remained so. He received many private and public commissions. He was wealthy, in spite of the fact that painters were relatively poorly paid in Holland. He went bankrupt; his beautiful house on St. Anthonies Breestraat and its contents were sold at auction in 1658; but this was because Rembrandt lived above his means and had made several risky investments. He was an unscrupulous businessman in a society that could be called capitalistic. He dealt in works that were not always his. He intervened in public auctions to support or raise the value of his works. After his bankruptcy he asked his companion Hendrickje and his son Titus to set up a corporation for the sale of his works, which secured him a comfortable income until he died. Rembrandt was a hard man in matters of money as in private matters. Saskia died in 1642. Rembrandt then lived with Geertje Dircks, but he threw her out of his house in 1649 and went to court several times against her, not to mention obscure matters of inheritance. Hendrickje Stoffels, who was twenty years younger than Rembrandt, then became his common-law wife, and he never married her in spite of the scandal caused by this situation.

Rembrandt kept receiving commissions for portraits, and this was a good indicator of his social rank. Like the aristocrats during the preceding political regime, the Dutch bourgeois wished to have their portraits painted for posterity. There was also a type of portrait peculiar to Dutch society: the group portrait. Aside from government institutions, there were many civic and professional associations that were just as significant for the workings of the state. These associations commissioned group portraits of their principal officials. Even Frans Hals, who painted twenty years before Rembrandt, made such paintings seem very solemn. Rembrandt's first commission of this sort, painted in 1632 when he arrived in Amsterdam, showed the same stiffness: *Doctor Nicolaes Tulp Demonstrating the Anatomy of the Arm* described Amsterdam's "surgeon general" giving a "lecture" to his colleagues (see pages 46-47). This ceremony was characteristic of Dutch bourgeois society: Every year, the surgeon general gave a public lecture, open to everyone who could pay to attend. Society was thus formally presenting one of its scientific institutions. The painting underscored the theatrical aspect of the ceremony, although Rembrandt tried to give some life to the solemn scene and break up the usual stiff composition of group portraits. The fact that Doctor Tulp alone wears a hat indicates his eminent status in the group. The eyes of his colleagues show the attention they give to his words, the significance of which he is stressing with a gesture of his hand. One of the onlookers holds a sheet of notes. Finally, a big open book on the right hand side of the picture points to the intellectual significance of the ceremony. All these elements were socially defined; they imposed strict constraints on the painting, but Rembrandt wished also to give some life to the composition. The painting is a transition work, where Rembrandt was both abiding by the rules and changing them. The faces of the onlookers are in the light while the surroundings are set in deep shadow; they are arranged in a triangle, the summit of which points to the face of the surgeon general. The viewer's attention is thus drawn to his face. And this movement of the eyes is reinforced by the horizontal line created by the corpse.

Ten years later, in 1642, Rembrandt painted *The Nightwatch*, a group portrait of very different artistic ambition (see pages 50-51). The painting has been rightly considered one of his masterpieces. It shows that Rembrandt was interested in the realities of contemporary society because they gave him an opportunity to elaborate his ideas as a painter. Each figure depicted here is a portrait, with unique features. The Rijksmuseum in Amsterdam gives it a more appropriate title, closer to the theme, that identifies the head of the group: *The Company of Captain Frans Banning Cocq*. These portraits, however, are anything but stiff. This company of Amsterdam's municipal guard is on the move. It has just crossed one of the city's doors, which can be seen faintly in the background of the painting. The scene is much more lively than it was in *Doctor Nicolaes Tulp Demonstrating the Anatomy of the Arm*, in which only the expression on the faces of the participants showed animation and the attention given to the professor's words. It could be suggested that Rembrandt chose to celebrate here the military feat of this company in 1641, when it took part in the defense of Amsterdam. The group portrait as a genre is taken beyond any static stiffness. Similarly, Rembrandt gave a lively expression to each portrait in the group. The representation of men in action took precedence over ostentatious staging. This development of the portrait, whether individual or in group, toward a more lively depiction befit the action-oriented ethics of the contemporary bourgeois society as well as the essential principles of humanism. Man is man inasmuch as he acts, as he, Descartes wrote, becomes "master and owner of nature." This was to bear consequences in the field of art, and history painting in particular. Whether they were the mighty of this world or saints, the figures that marked the course of history stopped being symbols of a Fate ruled by God's will. They were pictured as actors on a historical stage. The technique in *The Nightwatch* matched this idea of Man and made it a painter's idea. Before being shaped into a theme, this was a matter of work with paints

The Holy Family
in the Carpenter's Workshop, 1645
Pen and bistre, 6⁵⁄₁₆″ × 6³⁄₁₆″ (16 × 15.8 cm)
Musée Bonnat, Bayonne

Christ Crucified Between the Two Thieves, 1653
Etching I/IX, 15⅛″ × 17¹¹⁄₁₆″ (38.5 × 45 cm)
Staatliche Museen, Preußischer Kulturbesitz
Kupferstichkabinett, Berlin-Dahlem

and, most of all, a matter of chiaroscuro.
The title *The Nightwatch* is particularly
inept. The successive layers of protective
varnish and the natural aging process of
colors have made the tones darker. As
a consequence, it was believed in the
nineteenth century to be a night scene.
But night and day, light and shade in
Rembrandt's work, are not realistic effects
evoking the artist's experience of real life.
Before anything else, they are pictorial
effects. In this painting celebrating the
brave men under Captain Cocq, everything
is artificial chiaroscuro. The viewer
cannot be sure about the source of light;
there may even be several. There is
no clear reason why some parts of the
painting are hit by light and others are
not. There is no "realistic" explanation for
the light. The pictorial effect, however,
is significant. By spreading the light, the
painter forces the viewer to move his
eyes, and this movement gives a life to
the very movement of the men depicted

The Raising of the Cross, 1633
Black chalk and wash in India ink
9⅛" × 7⅜" (23.2 × 18.7 cm)
Nationalbibliothek, Vienna

in the painting. The scattered light attracts the viewer in several directions,
deep into a space bathed in semidarkness.

Rembrandt's technique expressed the core of his ideas, as is always the case for the
great artists. Maurice Denis aptly said in 1912, "Remember that a painting, before
it is a war horse, a female nude or some little genre scene, is primarily a flat surface
covered with colors arranged in a certain order."[1] The treatment of light, its order,
expresses the essential in Rembrandt's ideas. It underscores the fact that man's dynamic
vision gives objects their shape, especially when these objects are moving in a joyous
or dramatic confrontation. Either the technique of the chiaroscuro secures barely visible
transitions between places and things, which then seem to belong to a seamless space;
or it does the very opposite; light and shade are sharply opposed, and space is not
continuous but torn by empty spots. As he grew older, Rembrandt scattered light to
show the odd components in the experience of seeing, which works on different planes.
Rembrandt's paintings at the time of *The Nightwatch* were characterized by a great
intellectual tension, which was to diminish later. Here his eyes perceived the brightness

(1) Maurice Denis, *Théories (1890-1910): Du Symbolisme et de Gauguin vers un nouvel ordre classique.* Paris: Rouart & Watelin,
    1920. Reissued in part, *Théories.* Paris: Herman, 1964, p. 1.

THE RAISING OF THE CROSS, ca 1633.   Oil on canvas, 37⅞″ × 28⅜″ (96.2 × 72.2 cm)
Alte Pinakothek, Munich. Photo Artothek, Peissenberg

THE DESCENT FROM THE CROSS, 1633.   Oil on panel, 35⅛″ × 25⅝″ (89.4 × 65.2 cm)
Alte Pinakothek, Munich. Photo Artothek, Peissenberg

THE BLINDING OF SAMSON, 1636
Oil on canvas, 92¹⁵⁄₁₆″ × 118⅞″ (236 × 302 cm)
Städelsches Kunstinstitut, Frankfurt
Photo Blauel/Artothek, Peissenberg

of light; there they came against walls of darkness. There was always an anxiety in Rembrandt's mind; he was less preoccupied with the meaning of the reality he could perceive, its apparent truth or falseness, than with the presence itself of the things he could see, which was made so intense by contrary motions.

Rembrandt's depictions of men's actions expressed a similar anxious tension in terms of ethics. Real life could be exalting, but it was not kind, it was often made of sorrow. His pictures of Christian and biblical scenes could express some tenderness, such as *Christ at Emmaus* or *Resting During the Flight to Egypt* (1647, National Gallery of Ireland, Dublin) or *The Holy Family* (1646, The Hermitage Museum, Leningrad). The Gospel, however, also gave him themes for meditation on human violence. During the 1630s, Rembrandt painted a series of pictures of the stations of the Cross. He expressed his feelings of piety and sorrow by picturing himself at the right of Christ in *The Descent from the Cross* (1633, see page 57), as he had already featured himself by the saint in *The Martyrdom of St. Stephen*. What makes the depiction of Christ tragic is the rough texture of paints covering the crucified body with a network of scars, and the body dislocated by the hands that support it as they take it down from the cross. It was not the unthinkable in death that retained Rembrandt's attention, as it had Caravaggio's when he painted *The Death of the Virgin Mary* in 1603. His emotion was not caused by horror facing that which Bossuet called, quoting Tertullian, "this thing which does not have a name in any language." Rembrandt's vision, as in the etching *Christ Crucified Between the Two Thieves*, used the chiaroscuro to unite heavens and earth in the same stormy light: He could only conceive of the future of mankind and the world with a God both forgiving and terrifying (see page 54).

Rembrandt was struck on several occasions by the cruelty in the life of men. In his youth he was fascinated by destitute vagrants and beggars. In his old age, he was to be fascinated by the destruction of his own body. Before that, he sometimes focussed on such terrifying episodes from the Bible as the story of Samson and Delilah. One of the paintings in this series deals with the reality of torture, which must have been still cruelly fresh in the memory the Flemish people recently under Spanish dominion. In the Christian tradition the depiction of martyrdoms could present details of the torture inflicted on the saints. But Saint Sebastian pierced by arrows maintained a peaceful expression, as did Saint Stephen painted by Rembrandt in 1625. Arrows and stones were the symbolic attributes of the saints rather than deadly weapons. *The Triumph of Delilah*, also called *The Blinding of Samson*, was painted in 1636 (see page 58). The picture is almost unbearable. The soldier runs his dagger up to the hilt in Samson's eye socket; the eye is bursting; blood is spurting out. The body of the victim is twisting. His foot is bent back in a spasm. The scene is taking place in a cave that forms a deep shadow. The entrance of the cave lets in a stream of light. There, a figure bathed in light, with an angelic face and pastel-colored clothes, Delilah is leaving the cave. She turns around to look at her lover for the last time, while holding her long hair floating in the wind. The violent contrast between light and shade comes

SAMSON BETRAYED BY DELILAH, 1628. Oil on panel, 24⅛″ × 19⅝″ (61.4 × 50 cm)
Staatliche Museen, Preußischer Kulturbesitz, Gemäldegalerie, Berlin-Dahlem

Two Butchers at Work, ca 1635
Pen and bistre
5⅞" × 7⅞" (14.9 × 20 cm)
Städelsches Kunstinstitut, Frankfurt

with an inversion of values: Light is treason; the bloody red of pain takes the viewer to darkness. Unlike the suffering of Christ, this pain brings no salvation.

Rembrandt achieved a sort of serenity with age. How does a painter express serenity? It is less a choice to depict the peaceful side of life than a matter of perspective, similar to the viewer on the top of a mountain who can see both the fertile and barren land. At this stage in life Rembrandt did not bother to pass judgment anymore and was satisfied with observing the multiple aspects of reality, even when they were incompatible or contradictory. The two paintings he made of *The Slaughtered Ox* are indicative of this evolution. The first one, which is at the Art Gallery and Museum in Glasgow, features a whole staging. *The Slaughtered Ox* is hanging from the beams inside the slaughterhouse. A woman is washing off the blood stains on the floor. The severed head of the animal is on the floor, in the foreground, on the right hand side of the picture. Something happened and is still going on. The viewer may wonder about the painting's real theme. This oil on panel may be based on a drawing made in 1625, *Two Butchers Working on the Frame of an Animal*. Before Rembrandt, this theme was tied to the depiction of an episode from the Bible, when the father ordered that the fatted calf be killed to celebrate the return of the prodigal son. The architecture of the country slaughterhouse and the clothing of the woman were Rembrandt's manner of bringing this parable into contemporary times, as painters often did. The Dutch tradition, in particular, liked to see biblical scenes expressed through things of the familiar daily life, which were thus sanctified.

The second *Slaughtered Ox* (The Louvre Museum, Paris, see page 62) expressed a clearly different vision. The traces of action have almost vanished from the scene. With

The Slaughtered Ox, 1655.   Oil on panel, 36¹⁵⁄₁₆″ × 27⅛″ (94 × 69 cm)
Musée du Louvre, Paris. Photo Réunion des Musées Nationaux, Paris

them, the biblical meaning and also the meaning of some daily aspects of life have vanished as well. The severed head of the ox, the reminder of the butcher's deed, is not there anymore, on the ground. The woman is not washing away the blood that evoked the animal's agony. She is only peering from the door; she has ceased to be part of a story that could be told. She has become, like ourselves, a silent spectator. What is seen in the painting switches to something beyond words. Here hangs the frame of a skinned animal, and it needs no reference to a Biblical tale or the embellishment of daily life. It simply evokes the realization that man's flesh is nourished with animal flesh. This naked flesh in the painting is a metaphor for a deadly reality that leaves the viewer almost speechless. This is shown simply, through bare painting. Rembrandt put the body of the animal in the foreground, and it seems to fill the viewer's whole vision; the brush worked wide strokes in the thick paints, their violence a tangible metaphor for the nameless mass of muscles, fat, and bones. Both the biblical story and the pragmatism of the bourgeois Dutch have receded from the picture. The viewer is just facing the unspeakable. Leonardo da Vinci had expressed horror about eating: "Men and animals are only a track, a conduit for food, a burial for other birds, an inn for the dead." [1] But Vinci himself dissected many corpses of animals and men in order to make intelligible drawings. The artist reaches a stages where nothing visible is foreign to him, whether it is pleasing or terrifying. All artists feel the same astonishment about reality, made of admiration and anxiety. Later, Eugène Delacroix and Chaim Soutine were to take the theme of the *Slaughtered Ox*, and their paintings expressed the same astonishment facing the skinned flesh; their work with colors turned the paints into real flesh, and they made the viewer think of that flesh as a shapeless mass, both startling and fascinating. The visible world is shown as both bare and enigmatic.

The Slaughtered Ox at the Louvre is almost monochromatic, painted in reddish brown tones. The frame of the animal stands out in light tones against a background, the darkness of which is heightened by the fact that it contains almost no details that could serve as a description of a place. The viewer can only see the sharp contrast between the light on the animal shape and the background; this contrast creates the whole sense of space in the painting. Starting in the 1640s, Rembrandt created such subtle contrasts in the chiaroscuro that the vision becomes blurred. As he was growing older, he preferred uncertain subtlety to violently contrasting light and shade. *The Slaughtered Ox* at the Louvre stands out against the background. In many other works the subtle differences in the values of light blur the outlines and the depth of perspective. The most striking paintings show an undefined space with holes of light. It becomes difficult to decide, in the chiaroscuro, which parts are jutting out and which are receding. Light and shade are mixed with such subtlety that the spatial relationship between things becomes uncertain. An atmospheric perspective takes over linear perspective, dissolving the sense of depth. The imaginary space cannot be measured through an ideal

(1) Leonardo da Vinci, *Les Carnets de Léonard de Vinci*. Paris: Gallimard, 1942, vol. 1, p. 63 (Codex Atlanticus 76 v.a).

CHRIST AT EMMAUS, ca 1629
Oil on paper laid down on panel
14¹¹⁄₁₆″ × 16⅝″ (37.4 × 42.3 cm)
Musée Jacquemart-André, Paris

64

CHRIST AT EMMAUS, 1648
Oil on panel, 26¾″ × 25⁵⁄₁₆″ (68 × 65 cm)
Musée du Louvre, Paris
Photo Réunion des Musées Nationaux, Paris

THE DISGRACE OF AMAN, 1665. Oil on canvas, 49¹⁵⁄₁₆″ × 46¹⁄₁₆″ (127 × 117 cm)
Hermitage Museum, Leningrad. Photo Aurora Publishing, Leningrad

geometry. Rembrandt's art of the chiaroscuro makes the viewer survey the painting out of the boundaries of such mathematical measurements as proximity and distance, inside and outside, attraction and repulsion. The second version of *Christ at Emmaus*, painted in 1648, is one of the better examples of this optical experimentation and orientation of Rembrandt's ideas about representation. It is a striking, meaningful example. The effects of chiaroscuro establish a boundless relationship between Christ and his apostles, a mystical connection, a passionate relationship beyond the realm of reason. In the first version of *Christ at Emmaus* (1629, see page 64), the contrasts of light are very sharp. The silhouette of Christ in the foreground stands out like a figure in shadow theater against a light, the hidden source of which is somewhere between Christ's body and the apostle. The dramatic effect of this contrast is heightened by another one, created by the maid bending over her work against a second light. In the version dated 1648, no definite source of light can be detected. Light seems to surge from bodies and things. The more brilliant light is on the white tablecloth. But it penetrates the whole painting without marking any distinct direction. Rembrandt's treatment of light and shade expresses the many incompatible aspects of that which is visible. The architecture of the room is itself blurred, the vault above the figure of Christ is another deep shadow (see page 65).

Rembrandt suggested a space where neither the size of things, their texture, or their color mattered. Things were there as a more intense vibration of light. In spite of the presence of a number of objects in the painting, such a space creates an expanse, the boundaries of which remain uncertain. Because it is a modulation of vibrating light, the space of the painting becomes the lively metaphor for a universe viewed as infinite. The followers of Poussin, who gave pride of place to lines, were soon to battle in various academies against the followers of Rubens, who advocated an art based on the preeminence of colors. But one of the best theoreticians of art who took part in this debate, Roger de Piles,[1] perceived correctly that Rembrandt was working on another level. He praised him for "his supreme intelligence in the technique of the chiaroscuro." Rembrandt's chiaroscuro was indeed a new step in the history of painting. Leonardo da Vinci used the sfumato to reconcile linear perspective and color perspective. Caravaggio sharply opposed light and shade. Rembrandt neither reconciled nor accentuated the two contradictory terms. Thus he created a space that is infinite, or at least unmeasurable, by which the act of seeing becomes an event rather than a mere registering of that which is visible. To see and to make one see is to pull something out of the shadow where one's vision is lost. A new world is born each time the viewer sees Rembrandt's light. Christian contemporaries of Rembrandt read this as the expression of a mystical union, as St. John of the Cross said that God's light took him into the darkness of night. But artistic theory is rarely of a religious order; Rembrandt's reality belongs to this world as it appears through the light.

(1) Born in 1635, Roger de Piles was a writer and a diplomat as well as a painter. He played a significant role in the controversy about color and line that divided French artists under Louis XIV. He championed the work of Rubens and invented the word *clair-obscur* (chiaroscuro). He was elected at the Académie in 1699.

SIMEON WITH THE CHRIST CHILD IN THE TEMPLE, ca 1666-1669
Oil on canvas, 38⅝″ × 31″ (98 × 79 cm).   Statens Konstmuseer, Stockholm

The Presentation in the Temple, 1661
Pen and brush in bistre, white body-color
4¹¹/₁₆″ × 3½″ (12 × 8.9 cm)
Koninklijke Bibliotheek, The Hague

In his maturity, and later in his older age, Rembrandt created works that were more than ever marked by his astonishment at that which kept appearing through the light. He shed most accessory details that could give indications of the circumstances of an event or a tale. Even in his history paintings, he moved away from the narrative role of objects in order to express his strong wordless reaction to the intense presence of these objects. *The Disgrace of Aman* shows three figures whose turbans indicate that the scene is taking place in the Middle East (1665, see page 66). But the only clue to the theme of the painting is in the title. In the last painting by Rembrandt, *Simon with the Child Christ at the Temple* (1669), only three faces are visible, which could be an allegory for the three stages in life. The play of light and shade blurs the details in favor of the faces and bodies of the figures in action (see page 68). *The Conspiracy of Claudius Civilis: The Oath* (1661) shows the staging in a painting dissolved by shining light (see page 25). *The Syndics of the Drapers' Guild* (1662) is a work in which the viewer's perception of space is oriented by the light streaming from the left and the cubic shape of the room where the association is meeting. But the brush stroke and the texture of the paints create a blurring effect. The men's features lack precision, their hair forms vague halos around their heads, and their faces bear expressions of surprise, as if they were astonished by Rembrandt's vision (see page 70).

With time Rembrandt painted fewer group portraits and history paintings. One of his most significant works, *The Jewish Bride* (ca 1666, see page 72) led to many speculations about its actual meaning. This was not the first time: *The Slaughtered Ox* was believed to refer to the tale of the prodigal son rather than to the scene described in the title. The picture may be of Isaac and Rebecca spied upon by Abimelech. The seventeenth-century clothes do not exclude references to the Bible. Aside from genre scenes in which daily life and work were depicted, the artists of the time gave a meaning to their pictures by turning them into illustrations of historic events or biblical stories.

THE SYNDICS OF THE DRAPER'S GUILD, 1662
Oil on canvas
75⅜″ × 109¾″ (191.5 × 279 cm)
Rijksmuseum
Amsterdam

70

Three Syndics ("de Staalmeesters"), ca 1662
Reed pen and bistre, wash, white body-color
6¹³/₁₆" × 8¹/₁₆" (17.3 × 20.5 cm)
Staatliche Museen, Preußischer Kulturbesitz
Kupferstichkabinett, Berlin-Dahlem

THE JEWISH BRIDE, ca 1666
Oil on canvas
47¹³⁄₁₆″ × 65½″ (121.5 × 166.5 cm)
Rijksmuseum, Amsterdam

The Jewish Bride, 1635
Pen, India ink and wash
12⅝″ × 7³⁄₁₆″ (32.2 × 18.2 cm)
Statens Konstmuseer, Stockholm

DANAE, ca 1636
Oil on canvas, 72⅝″ × 79¹⁵⁄₁₆″ (185 × 203 cm)
Hermitage Museum, Leningrad
Photo Aurora Publishing, Leningrad

73

Susanna Bathing, 1636
Oil on panel
18⁹⁄₁₆″ × 15³⁄₁₆″ (47.2 × 38.6 cm)
Mauritshuis, The Hague

Susanna Surprised by the Elders, 1647
Oil on panel, 30¹⁄₁₆″ × 36⁹⁄₁₆″ (76.6 × 92.7 cm)
Staatliche Museen, Preußischer Kulturbesitz
Gemäldegalerie, Berlin-Dahlem

Rembrandt, however, erased most signs indicating the circumstances of the story he depicted, and he made the painting timeless. The couple in *The Jewish Bride* is living outside of time in spite of their clothes. The love of this man and woman has a timeless quality. The position of the bodies, bent toward one another, the movement of their hands, both touching and pushing away, could as well be ours. Their eyes could also be ours, that appear not to see, eyes that are not seeking one another, as if to express that these two lovers are on the eve of desire, in the timeless moment of budding love.

A painting is always born from the desire in the artist's eyes, which accounts for the fact that the shining light in Rembrandt's work imparts such intensity to the presence of everything. This intensity grows when the theme of the painting is the painter's desire for a woman's body. Rembrandt painted many female nudes. He often followed the custom of the time and staged these nudes in stories drawn from the Bible or Greek mythology. This was how the nude body of men and women could be painted at the beginning of the Renaissance in Italy, when the human body could become an object of reflection in humanist philosophy. In 1636 Rembrandt painted *Danae* (see page 73). Here again there are questions about the interpretation of this painting. It might be Rachel waiting for Jacob, or Sarah expecting Abraham. The winged child featured above the woman lying on her bed could be an angel or the little god Eros. Greek mythology and tradition in painting had it that Zeus came to Danae in the shape of a golden rain. The figure coming through the door in the background seems to be dressed in contemporary clothes. One may wonder whether the painting evoked ancient tales. It remains that this is the picture of a naked woman, wearing bracelets, leaning on one elbow, and smiling to welcome her lover. Her intense presence derives, as always in Rembrandt's paintings, from the combination of light and shade. This combination is meant to express the coupling and mutual attraction between different people and things, rather than mark their location in a specific space. The size of the room is undetermined because it seems absorbed by deep shadows, where the woman's naked body shines, as well as the winged child, the man's face, a red rug, and the carved corner of a piece of furniture. This space cannot be measured, and the scene cannot be placed in time.

Paintings in which Rembrandt clearly indicated the setting of the scene can also have this timeless erotic quality. In *Susanna Bathing*, painted in 1636, the woman is spied upon by an old man and she tries to hide her nakedness with both hands (see page 74). In *Susanna Surprised by the Elders*, painted in 1647, one of the old men grabs her shirt (see page 75). The interpretation of these two pictures is clear. Something, however, takes the paintings out of their legendary context and time. In both paintings, Susanna looks at the viewer with fear in her eyes. She is afraid of the viewer, of us. Her eyes make us into voyeurs, like the two old men. In order to capture the viewer's interest, paintings need to offer the world to see, even things other than a naked body. Whatever the place, circumstances, and time, art's relationship with reality is based on a kind of voyeurism.

SARAH WAITING FOR TOBIT (WOMAN IN BED), ca 1649-1650
Oil on canvas, 31¹³⁄₁₆″ × 26⁹⁄₁₆″ (81.1 × 67.8 cm).   National Gallery of Scotland, Edinburgh

A Woman Bathing (Hendrickje Stoffels?), 1654
Oil on panel, 24¼″ × 18½″ (61.8 × 47 cm).   National Gallery, London

Female Nude Seated on a Chair
(seen from behind), 1654-1656
Pen and brush in bistre, on brownish paper
8¹¹⁄₁₆" × 7¼" (22.2 × 18.5 cm)
Staatliche Graphische Sammlung, Munich

Female Nude in Front of a Curtain, 1661
Pen, ink, and bistre
11¹¹⁄₁₆" × 7⅝" (29.8 × 19.3 cm)
The British Museum
London

A Girl Sleeping
(Study after Hendrickje), 1655-1656
Brush and bistre, wash
9¹¹⁄₁₆" × 8" (24.5 × 20.3 cm)
The Britisch Museum, London

Male Nude Standing, ca 1646
Pen and bistre, wash, heightened with white
body-color, over traces of red and black chalk
9¹⁵/₁₆″ × 7⅞″ (25.2 × 19.3 cm)
The British Museum, London

With time, Rembrandt progressively erased the circumstantial components of events and reality prominent in man's mind. He painted *Saskia as Flora* several times, in 1634 (see page 45), in 1635 (National Gallery, London), and in 1641 (Gemäldegalerie, Dresden). In 1633 he painted *Saskia with a Veil* (Rijksmuseum, Amsterdam), and in 1634 a *Portrait of Saskia* (National Gallery of Art, Washington, D.C.). Rembrandt put in references to mythology, the veil, the necklace, because he wished to pull the woman's beauty out of daily life. The references and ornaments, however, raise all sorts of dreams between the woman and the viewer. Around 1650, Rembrandt painted *Sarah Waiting for Tobit*, with Hendrickje half-naked (see page 77). In 1654, Hendrickje wears a shirt in *A Woman Bathing*, which she pulls up high on her thighs (see page 78). And the greatest nakedness is not the woman's: It is the naked painting, the brush work in the thick paints that attracts the viewer, as well as this great vertical line of light against a background that is almost black in places. Rembrandt produced several drawings during the same period in which there were no mythological references

Female Nude Sleeping
ca 1657-1658
Drawing, pen, brush, bistre and wash
5⁷/₁₆″ × 11⅛″ (13.7 × 28.4 cm)
Rijksprintenkabinett, Amsterdam

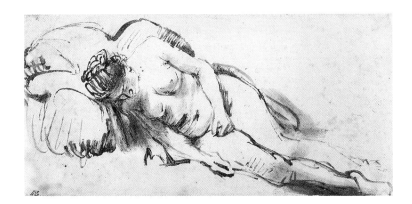

Bathshaba with King David's Letter, 1654
Oil on canvas
55⅝″ × 55⅝″ (142 × 142 cm)
Musée du Louvre, Paris
Photo Réunion des Musées Nationaux, Paris

SELF-PORTRAIT, ca 1629
Oil on panel, 14⅞″ × 11⅜″ (37.9 × 28.9 cm)
Mauritshuis, The Hague

or ornaments. Like his portraits, *Female Nude Seated on a Chair (Seen from Behind)*, *Female Nude Sleeping*, and *Female Nude (Surrounded by a Drapery)* show us that the Renaissance man is most sensitive of all to the other's body (see page 79).

Something very moving happened in Rembrandt's work. During his whole life he had observed his own body as if it were independent from him, as if it were another's. Between 1620 and 1669, when he died, he produced ninety self-portraits, without counting the instances when he pictured himself in his history paintings. He observed himself more patiently than he observed anybody else. He wore costumes, he made faces in front of the mirror, he posed. His youthful portraits often wore a defiant, insolent expression. His portraits as an old man showed a different insolence, an irony about himself and others. But what was he seeking while spending so many hours and days, each year, scrutinizing himself in the mirror and painting his own portrait? Was he moved by a need for psychological introspection? Did he paint so many portraits of others out of a similar curiosity for the psychology of his models? The *Self-Portrait* at the Mauritshuis at The Hague shows him with the arrogance of the twenty-year-old (1629, see page 82). The one at the

SELF-PORTRAIT, ca 1668
Oil on canvas, 38⅜″ × 25⁵⁄₁₆″ (82.5 × 65 cm)
Wallraf-Richartz Museum, Cologne

SELF-PORTRAIT, ca 1630
Oil on panel, 27⅜″ × 22⅜″ (69.7 × 57 cm)
National Museums and Galleries on Merseyside, Walker Art Gallery, Liverpool

Self-Portrait. Portrait of the Artist with a Cap and Golden Chain, 1633
Oil on panel, 27½″ × 20¹³⁄₁₆″ (70 × 53 cm). Musée du Louvre, Paris
Photo Réunion des Musées Nationaux, Paris

SELF-PORTRAIT, 1652
Oil on canvas, 44⅛″ × 32″ (112 × 81.5 cm)
Kunsthistorisches Museum, Vienna

SELF-PORTRAIT, ca 1657
Oil on panel
19⁵⁄₁₆″ × 16⅛″ (49.2 × 41 cm)
Kunsthistorisches Museum
Vienna

Wallraf-Richartz Museum in Cologne features the face of a decrepit old man smirking (1668, see page 82). In the last one he painted, which hangs at the National Gallery in London, he rises shortly before dying, staring at his own swollen face (1669, see page 89). The discovery of one's mind, or the mind of others, seems unimportant compared to the naked truth about the aging of the body and its implicit mask of death. Eroticism, the desire for another body, is one of the forces of life. The other force is the one that leads to the death of the body. This is how the body of the painter who observes himself in a mirror becomes another.

Rembrandt's long series of self-portraits revealed his goals better than his other works. The thoughtful part of art derives from the artist's astonishment that reality should exist, and that it should be different from anything one knows, even when he is painting his own face. Philosophy in art confronts destiny as an enigma without an answer. Rembrandt's perpetual confrontation with the enigma of the world is played out among streaks of light shining through the shadow, like fragments of knowledge emerging from ignorance. This confrontation exists in all arts. The poet Stéphane Mallarmé was wondering about the enigma created by the existence or absence of a meaning in one of his poems. He then said of this "rather cabalistic" sonnet something which could be said of every painting by Rembrandt, "It is as black-and-white as possible and it seems to lend itself to an etching of dreams and void." [1]

(1) Stéphane Mallarmé, Letter to Cazalis dated July 1868. Paris: Gallimard, Ed. de la Pléiade, p. 1484.

Self-Portrait. Study for the Painting now at the
Louvre Museum, Paris, dated 1660
Reed pen, India ink, and wash
3¼" × 2¾" (8.2 × 7 cm)
Österreichische Nationalbibliothek, Vienna

Self-Portrait. Portrait of the Artist at His Easel, 1660
Oil on canvas, 43¹¹⁄₁₆″ × 35⅜″ (111 × 90 cm)
Musée du Louvre, Paris. Photo Réunion des Musées Nationaux, Paris

SELF-PORTRAIT, 1669
Oil on canvas, 33¾″ × 27¹¹⁄₁₆″ (86 × 70.5 cm)
National Gallery, London

BIOGRAPHY

1606   Rembrandt Harmenszoon van Rijn was born on July 15, at Leyden in the Netherlands, the seventh child of Harmen Geritszoon van Rijn and Cornelia Willemsdochter van Zuybroeck.

1613-1620   Studied at the Latin School in Leyden.

1620   On May 20, he enrolled at the University of Leyden but he left after a few months.

1621-1623   Apprenticeship in the studio of the painter Jakob van Swanenburg, in Leyden.

1624   Stay in Amsterdam. He worked under Pieter Lastman, a highly regarded painter who had spent a few years in Rome and knew the works of the great Italian Renaissance artists.

1625   Return to Leyden. He painted his first known work: *The Martyrdom of St. Stephen*. First etchings.

1626   It is believed that Rembrandt shared his studio for a time with Jan Lievens, also a former student of Lastman. The two artists certainly influenced one another, and Lievens introduced Rembrandt to the Utrecht and Haarlem schools.

1627   He discovered the series of etchings by Callot, *The Beggars*.

1628   Gérard Dou became his student. Rembrandt began to paint head studies when he had his first students. Portraits of his mother. Constantin Huygens, the secretary of Stathouder Frederic-Henry of Nassau and father of the famous physicist Christiaan Huygens, became a fervent supporter of Rembrandt and Jan Lievens. He mentioned Rembrandt in his "Diary," one of the few accounts on Rembrandt's personality and his attitude toward work. First self-portraits.

1631   Rembrandt settled in Amsterdam, while Lievens left for England. He took a share in the art business of Hendrick van Uylenburg, in whose house he was living. He began a major career as a portrait painter and received commissions from the urban aristocracy and the great bourgeoisie, whether they were Calvinists, Mennonites, Remonstrants, or Catholics. He painted about forty portraits between 1631 and 1640.

1632   The surgeon general of Amsterdam, Professeur Nicolaes Tulp, gave a public lecture in anatomy, which Rembrandt was to commemorate in a painting.

1633   First portraits of Saskia. First commissions from Prince Frederic-Henry (*The Raising of the Cross*, *The Descent from the Cross*), who, for twenty years, was to be one of Rembrandt's best clients.

1634   He married Saskia van Uylenburg, his partner's niece, born in 1612. The couple lived in the house of Jakob van Uylenburg. *Saskia as Flora*. Saskia brought in the marriage a fortune of about 40,700 guilders. Rembrandt became a member of the painters' guild of Saint Luke and he took apprentices. Irrespective of the guild's rules, he conceived of his studio as an academy of fine arts and took more than three students at the time.

1634   The City of Amsterdam commissioned three paintings on the Passion of Christ. Rembrandt and his wife settled in a house on Nieuwe Doelenstraat.

1635   A first child was born, Rumbertus, who died the following year.

1636   First landscape: *Landscape with the Baptism of the Eunuch*.

1638   A girl was born, Cornelia, who died also.

1639   Rembrandt and his wife moved to a house on Zwanenburgerstraat. He saw at an auction the *Portrait of Baltassare Castiglione* and the *Portrait of Ariosto* by Titian. In May, Rembrandt and his wife settled in a big house on St. Anthonies Breestraat, which he paid thirteen thousand guilders. He was never able to reimburse the debts incurred when he bought this house. Rembrandt resumed painting portraits of the urban aristocrats and rich merchants, as well as members of his circle.

1640   A second daughter was born, also named Cornelia, who died shortly thereafter. Rembrandt's mother died. Peter Mundy published "The Travels of Peter Mundy in Europe and Asia," in which he praised Rembrandt. The former burgomaster of Leyden, Johannes Orles, published the first biography of Rembrandt in "Beschrijvinge der Staat Leyden."

1641   Birth of his son Titus. Death of Titia van Loo; she was Saskia's sister, to whom she was very close.

1642   *The Nightwatch*. On June 14, Saskia died from tuberculosis. Rembrandt was deeply shaken and his production waned. Geertje Dircks was hired as a governess. She became Rembrandt's mistress.

1648   Rembrandt took Geertje Dircks to court and accused her of having sold Saskia's jewels which he had given her as a gift.

1649   Hendrickje Stoffels, born in 1625 or 1626, came to live in Rembrandt's house and became his mistress. He will never marry her, and the reason may be that he did not want to risk losing an annuity inherited from Saskia.

1650   Many drypoint landscapes.

1653   Rembrandt started to have financial difficulties as a result of some risky investments. He mortgaged all his possessions. First commission from the Italian collector, Don Antonio Ruffo.

1654   Rembrandt and Hendrickje were called before an ecclesiastical court and accused of concubinage. Hendrickje gave birth to a daughter named Cornelia.

1656   Ever more in debt, Rembrandt tried and failed to put his house under his son's name. Titus was given another guardian. An inventory of Rembrandt's possessions was made in view of an auction.

1657   Titus made a will in favor of Hendrickje and her daughter Cornelia. Rembrandt's possessions were sold at auction.

1659   Rembrandt devoted the last ten years of his life almost exclusively to painting and drawing.

1660   A legal arrangement made Hendrickje and Titus the owners of Rembrandt's work, in charge of selling it. Rembrandt settled in a modest house on Rozengracht with Hendrickje, Titus, and Cornelia. He built up a new art collection.

1661   Hendrickje fell very ill and made a will in favor of Cornelia and Titus. Rembrandt was named their guardian.

1661-1662   *The Conspiracy of Claudius Civilis*.

1663   Death of Hendrickje.

1666   *Isaac and Rebecca (The Jewish Bride)*.

1668   In February, Titus married Magdalena van Loo. He died the following September.

1669   Birth of Tita, the daughter of Titus. Rembrandt died on October 4.

Two Negroes, 1661.   Oil on canvas, 30%16″ × 25⅜″ (77.8 × 64.5 cm)
Mauritshuis, The Hague

BIBLIOGRAPHY

CATALOGUES RAISONNÉS

BARTSCH, A. von. *Catalogue raisonné de toutes les estampes qui forment l'œuvre de Rembrandt, et ceux de ses principaux imitateurs.* Vienna, 1797.

BENESCH, O. *The Drawings of Rembrandt. A Critical and Chronological Catalogue.* 6 vols. Revised and completed by Eva Benesch. London: Phaidon; New York: Praeger, 1973.

BLANC, C. *L'Œuvre complet de Rembrandt.* 2 vols. Paris, 1859-1861.

BODE, W. von. *The Complete Works of Rembrandt.* I-VIII. Paris, 1897-1906.

BOON, K. G. *Rembrandt de etser: het volledige werk.* Amsterdam, 1977.

BREDIUS, A. *Rembrandt. The complete edition of the paintings.* Revised by Horst Gerson. London: Phaidon, 1969.

CLAUSSIN, C. de. *Catalogue raisonné de toutes les estampes qui forment l'œuvre de Rembrandt, et des principales pièces de ses élèves.* Paris 1824. Supplement 1828.

DAULBY, D. *A Descriptive Catalogue of the Works of Rembrandt and of his Scholars, Bol, Livens, and van Vliet, Compiled from the Original Etchings and from the Catalogues of de Burgy, Gersaint, Helle and Glomy, Marcus and Yver.* Liverpool, 1796.

DUTUIT, E. *L'Œuvre complet de Rembrandt.* Paris, London, Leipzig, 1883, Supplement 1885.

GERSAIN, G., HELLE and GLOMY. *Catalogue raisonné de toutes les pièces qui forment l'œuvre de Rembrandt.* Paris, 1751.

HIND, A. M. *A Catalogue of Rembrandt's Etchings.* London 1923.

HOFSTEDE DE GROOT, C. *Die Handzeichnungen Rembrandts. Versuch eines beschreibenden und kritischen Katalogs.* Haarlem, 1906.

LECALDANO, P. *The Complete Paintings of Rembrandt.* London, 1973.

MIDDLETON, C. H. *A Descriptive Catalogue of the Etched Work of Rembrandt.* London, 1878.

MÜNZ, L. *Rembrandt's Etchings.* 2 vols. London: Phaidon, 1952.

ROVINSKI, D. *L'Œuvre gravé de Rembrandt.* Saint Petersburg, 1890. Supplement, 1914.

SALOMON, H. *Catalogo completo dell'opera grafica di Rembrandt.* Milan, 1972.

WHITE, C. and BOON, K. G. *Rembrandt's Etchings, a new critical catalogue.* Amsterdam, London, New York, 1969.

WORKS ON REMBRANDT

ALPERS, S. *Rembrandt's Enterprise. The Studio and the Market.* Chicago, 1988.

BAILEY, A. *Rembrandt's House: Exploring the World of the Great Master.* Boston, London, 1978.

BAUCH, K. *Die Kunst des jungen Rembrandt.* Heidelberg, 1933.

BAUCH, K. *Der frühe Rembrandt une seine Zeit. Studien zur geschichtlichen Bedeutung seines Frühstils.* Berlin, 1960.

BAUCH, K. *Die Nachtwache.* Stuttgart, 1957.

BAUCH, K. *Rembrandt Gemälde.* Berlin, 1966.

BECK, M. D. *Der junge Rembrandt und Italien. Zur Herleitung und Verarbeitung der italienischen Motive im Frühwerk Rembrandts.* Doctoral dissertation, Bonn, 1949.

BENESCH, O. *Rembrandt. Werk und Forschung.* Vienna, 1935. Revised by Eva Benesch, Lucerne, 1970.

BENESCH, O. *Rembrandt. Zeichnungen.* London, 1947.

BENESCH, O. *Rembrandt.* Geneva, 1957.

BENESCH, O. *Rembrandt als Zeichner.* Geneva, Cologne, 1963.

BENRHARD, M. *Rembrandt. Vol. 1: Druckgraphik. Vol. 2: Handzeichnungen.* Munich, 1976.

BJÖRKLUND, G. *Rembrandt's Etchings. True and False.* London, Stockholm, New York, 1955.

BOCKEMÜHL, M. *Rembrandt: zum Wandel des Bildes und seiner Anschauung im Spätwerk.* Mittenwald, 1981.

BODE, W. von. *Rembrandt. Beschreibendes Verzeichnis seiner Gemälde mit den heliographischen Nachbildungen.* Paris, 1897-1905.

BODE, W. von. *Rembrandt und seine Zeitgenossen. Charakterbilder der großen Meister der holländischen und flämischen Malerschule im siebzehnten Jahrhundert.* Leipzig, 1906.

BODE, W. and VALENTINER, W. *Rembrandt in Bild und Wort.* Berlin, undated. [1907].

BOLTEN, J. *Rembrandt.* Wiesbaden, 1977.

BOLTEN, J. and BOLTEN-REMPT, H. *The Hidden Rembrandt.* Milan, Chicago, 1977.

BOON, K. G. *"Rembrandt.f." Das graphische Werk.* Munich, Vienna, 1963.

BRAUNFELS, W. *Rembrandt. Leben und Werk.*BREDIUS, A. *Rembrandt Schilderijen.* Utrecht, 1935. *The Paintings of Rembrandt.* Vienna, 1936.

BRION, M. *Rembrandt.* Paris, 1940.

BROM, G. *Rembrandt in de literatuur.* Groningen, 1936.

BROOS, B. P. J. *Rembrandt Studies.* Utrecht, 1977.

BROOS, B. P. J. *Index to the Formal Sources of Rembrandt's Art.* Maarssen, 1977.

BRUYN, J. *Rembrandt's keuze van Bijbelse onderwerpen.* Utrecht, 1959.

CAMPBELL, C. *Studies in the Formal Sources of Rembrandt's Figure Composition.* Doctoral dissertation. London, 1971.

CLARK, K. *Rembrandt and the Italian Renaissance.* London, 1966.

COPPIER, A. C. *Les Eaux-fortes de Rembrandt.* Paris, 1917, 1922, 1929.

COPPLESTONE, T. *Rembrandt*. London, 1974.

CZOBOR, A. *Rembrandt und sein Kreis*. Budapest, 1969.

EMMENS, J. A. *Rembrandt en de regels van de kunst*. Doctoral dissertation. Utrecht, 1932.

EISLER, M. *Der alte Rembrandt*. Vienna, 1927.

ESTEBAN, C., RUDEL, J. and MONNERET, S. *Rembrandt*. New York, 1980.

FILED-KOK, J. P. *Rembrandt. Etchings and Drawings in the Rembrandt-House*. Maarssen, 1972.

FOWKES, C. *The Life of Rembrandt*. London, 1978.

FREISE, K., LILIENFELD, K. and WICHMANN, H. *Rembrandts Handzeichnungen. I: Rijksprentenkabinett zu Amsterdam; II: Kupferstichkabinett zu Berlin; III: Staatl. Kupferstichkabinett und Sammlung Friedrich August II. zu Dresden*. Parchim, 1912-1925.

FUCHS, R. H. *Rembrandt en Amsterdam*. Rotterdam, 1968.

GANTNER, J. *Rembrandt und die Verwandlung klassischer Formen*. Bern, Munich, 1964.

GELDER, H. E. van *Rembrandt*. Amsterdam [1955].

GERSON, H. *Rembrandt. Gemälde*. Gütersloh, 1969.

GERSON, H. *Rembrandt: La Ronde de nuit*. Fribourg, 1973.

GOLDSCHEIDER, L. *Rembrandt. Gemälde und Graphik*. Cologne, 1960.

GRAUL, R. *Rembrandt. Die Radierungen*. 2nd edition. Leipzig, 1923.

GRAUL, R. and FEIST, P. H. *Rembrandt. Handzeichnungen*. Leipzig, 1969.

GREEF, R. *Rembrandts Darstellungen der Tobiasheilung*. Stuttgart, 1907.

HAAK, B. *Rembrandt. Sein Leben, sein Werk, seine Zeit*. New York, Cologne, 1969.

HAAK, B. *Rembrandt Zeichnungen*. Cologne, 1974.

HAAK, B. *Rembrandt: Leben und Werk*. Cologne, 1976.

HAMANN, R. *Rembrandts Radierungen*. Berlin, 1906.

HAMANN, R. *Rembrandt*. Revised edition by R. Hamann-MacLean; notes by W. Sumowski. Berlin, 1948.

HANFSTAENGL, E. *Rembrandt Harmensz. van Rijn*. Munich, 1947.

HAUSMANN, M. *Der Mensch vor Gottes Angesicht: Rembrandt-Bilder*. Neukirchen-Vluyn, 1976.

HAVERKAMP BEGEMANN, E. *The Nightwatch*. Princeton, 1982.

HECKSCHER, W. S. *Rembrandt's Anatomy of Dr. Nicolaes Tulp*. New York, 1958.

HEILAND, S. and LÜDECKE, H. *Rembrandt und die Nachtwelt*. Leipzig, 1960.

HELD, J. S. *Paintings by Rembrandt*. New York, 1956.

HELD, J. S. *Rembrandt's "Aristotle" and Other Rembrandt Studies*. Princeton, 1969.

HELD, J. S. *Der blinde Tobias und seine Heilung in Darstellungen Rembrandts*. Heidelberg, 1980.

HELD, J. S. *Rembrandt Studien*. Leipzig, 1983.

HELLINGA, W. G. *Rembrandt fecit 1642*. Amsterdam, 1956.

HIJMANS, W., KUIPER, L. and VELS HEIJN, A. *Rembrandts Nachtwacht: het vendel van Frans Banning Cocq, de geschiedenis van een schilderij*. Leyden, 1976.

HIND, A. M. *Rembrandt*. Cambridge, 1932, 1938.

HOFF, U. *Rembrandt und England*. Doctoral dissertation. Hamburg, 1935.

HOFSTEDE DE GROOT, C. *Rembrandts Bibel*. Amsterdam [1911].

JAHN, J. *Rembrandt*. Leipzig, 1956.

JANTZEN, H. *Rembrandt*. Bielefeld, Leipzig, 1923.

KEUTNER, H. A. F. *Rembrandts Hundertguldenblatt*. Doctoral dissertation. Cologne, 1950.

KITSON, M. *Rembrandt*. London, 1969.

KITSON, M. *Rembrandt*. Oxford, 1982.

KLUCKERT, E. *Rembrandt. Von der Themenvielfalt der Kunst*. Pliezhausen, 1982.

KNUTTEL, G. *Rembrandt. De meester en zijn werk*. Amsterdam, 1956.

KOCK, E. *Dein Kleid ist Licht, Rembrandt malt das Glauben*. Limbourg, 1977.

KOOT, T. *Rembrandt's Nightwatch: A Fascinating Story*. Amsterdam, 1969.

LANDSBERGER, F. *Rembrandt, the Jews and the Bible*. Philadelphia, 1946.

MARTIN, W. *De Hollandsche schilderkunst in de zeventiende eeuw. Rembrandt en zijn tijd*. Amsterdam, 1936, 1942.

MARTIN, W. *Van Nachtwacht tot feststoet*. Amsterdam, 1947.

MARZLUF, A. *Selbstbewußtsein als Bildkategorie: das Selbstbildnis bei Rembrandt*. Doctoral dissertation. Frankfurt, 1978.

MEYER, R. *Das Werk Rembrandts in Auffassung und Beurteilung von seinen Zeitgenossen bis heute*. Doctoral dissertation. Hamburg, 1924.

MICHEL, E. *Rembrandt. Sa vie, son œuvre, son temps*. Paris, 1893.

MÜLLER, J. E. *Rembrandt*. Paris, 1968.

MÜNZ, L. *Rembrandt*. Cologne, 1967.

MUTHER, R. *Rembrandt. Ein Künstlerleben*. Berlin, 1904.

NAGLER, G. K. *Leben und Werke des Malers und Radierers Rembrandt van Rijn*. Munich, 1843.

NEUMANN, C. *Rembrandt. Handzeichnungen*. Munich, 1918.

NEUMANN, C. *Rembrandt*. Munich, 1924.

NORDENFALK, G. *The Batavians' Oath of Allegiance. Rembrandt's only Monumental Painting*. Stockholm, 1982.

PERRY, B. A. S. *The Eastern Motif in the Works of Rembrandts*. Doctoral dissertation. Syracuse, 1980.

PILES, R. de. *Abrégé de la vie des peintres*. Paris, 1715.

PINDER, W. *Rembrandts Selbstbildnisse*. Königstein im Taunus, Leipzig, 1943, 1950.

PRINZ H. *Das Thema des weiblichen Aktes in Meister- und Schülerzeichnungen aus Rembrandts Spätzeit.* Doctoral dissertation. Marburg, 1946.

ROBERTS, K. *Rembrandt: Master Drawings.* Oxford, 1976.

ROSENBERG, J. *Rembrandt.* Cambridge, Massachusetts, 1948. New edition, *Rembrandt, Life and Work.* London, 1964.

ROSENBERG, J. *Rembrandt, Life and Work.* New York, 1980.

ROTTERMUND, H. M. *Rembrandts Handzeichnungen und Radierungen zur Bibel.* Stuttgart, 1963.

ROUIR, E. *Europäische Graphik im 17. Jahrhundert: Rembrandt und seine Zeitgenossen.* Stuttgart, 1974.

RYCKEVORSEL, J. L. A. A. M. van. *Rembrandt en de traditie.* Rotterdam, 1922.

SCHEIDIG, W. *Rembrandt als Zeichner.* Leipzig, 1962.

SCHWARTZ, G. *Rembrandt: All the Etchings Reproduced in True Size.* Maarssen, 1977.

SCHWARTZ, G. *Rembrandt; sijn leven, sijn schilderijnen.* Maarssen, 1984.

SEIDLITZ, W. von. *Die Radierungen Rembrandts.* Leipzig, 1922.

SIMMEL, G. *Rembrandt, ein kunstphilosophischer Versuch.* Leipzig, 1919.

SIMSON, O. von and KELCH J. *Neue Beiträge zur Rembrandt-Forschung.* Berlin, 1973.

SLATKES, L. J. *Rembrandt and Persia.* New York, 1983.

SLIVE, S. *Rembrandt and His Critics, 1630-1730.* The Hague, 1953.

SLIVE, S. *Drawings of Rembrandt.* New York, 1965.

SMIDT-DÖRRENBERG, I. *David und Saul, Variationen über ein Thema von Rembrandt.* Vienna, 1969.

STRAUSS, W. and MEULEN, M. van der. *The Rembrandt Documents.* New York, 1979.

SUMOWSKI, W. *Rembrandts Handzeichnungen.* Doctoral dissertation. Berlin, 1956.

TÜMPEL, C. *Rembrandt.* Antwerp, Paris, 1986.

VIS, D. *Rembrandt en Geertje Dircx.* Haarlem, 1965.

VOGEL KÖHN, D. *Rembrandts Kinderzeichnungen.* Cologne, 1981.

VOSMAER, C. *Rembrandt. Sa vie et ses œuvres.* The Hague, 1977.

WHITE, C. *Rembrandt and His World.* London, 1964.

WHITE, C. *Rembrandt as an Etcher. A Study of the Artist at Work.* London, 1969.

WRIGHT, C. *Rembrandt and His Art.* London, 1975.

YOUNG MAN HOLDING A FLOWER
ca 1665-1669
Pen drawing and bistre
6⅞″ × 4⅝″ (17.5 × 11.8 cm)
Musée du Louvre, Paris. Cabinet des Dessins

EXHIBITIONS

1956 *Rembrandt. Schilderijen.* Rijkmuseum, Amsterdam. Museum Boymans-van Beuningen, Rotterdam.

1964-1965 *Bijbelse Inspiratie. Tekeningen en prenten van Lucas van Leyden en Rembrandt.* Rijksmuseum, Amsterdam.

1968 *Rembrandt zeichnet.* Kupferstichkabinett der Staatlichen Museen, Berlin-Dahlem.

1969 *Rembrandt. Paintings and Drawings from European and Other Collections.* Rijksmuseum, Amsterdam.

1969 *Rembrandt-Graphik und Malerei der Rembrandt-Schule.* Bode Museum, Berlin.

1969 *Rembrandt van Rijn Radierungen.* Kunsthalle, Bielefeld.

1969 *Rembrandt: Experimental Etcher.* Museum of Fine Arts, Boston. The Pierpont Morgan Library, New York.

1969 *Rembrandt und seine Zeitgenossen.* Landesmuseum, Darmstadt.

1969 *Rembrandt, die Radierungen im Dresdner-Kupferstich-kabinett.* Staatliche Kunstsammlungen, Dresden.

1969 *Rembrandt and His Pupils.* Gallery of Fine Arts, Montreal. Art Gallery of Ontario, Toronto.

1969 *Exhibitions of works by Rembrandt, Paintings, Drawings, and Etchings.* Pushkin Museum, Moscow.

1969-1970 *Rembrandt after Three Hundert Years. An Exhibition of Rembrandt and His Followers.* The Art Institute, Chicago. The Minneapolis Institute of Arts. The Detroit Institute of Arts.

1970 *Rembrandt et son temps ; Dessins, des collections publiques et privées conservées en France.* Musée du Louvre, Paris.

1974 *Dutch Couples. Rembrandt and His Contemporaries.* Institute of Fine Arts, Cincinnati.

1975 *Rembrandt et la Bible.* Musée national Message biblique Marc Chagall, Nice.

1976 *Eaux-fortes de Rembrandt, 1606-1669, de la collection Thomas Dobrée.* Musée Dobrée, Nantes.

1979 *Rembrandt and the Bible.* Metropolitan Museum of Art, New York.

1980-1981 *Gods, Saints and Heroes ; Dutch Paintings in the Age of Rembrandt.* National Gallery of Art, Washington, D. C. The Detroit Institute of Arts. Rijksmuseum, Amsterdam.

1981 *Rembrandt. De Eendracht van het land.* Museum Boymans-van Beuningen, Rotterdam.

1981 *Work in Progress: Rembrandt. Etchings in Different States, All the Paintings.* Rembrandthuis, Amsterdam.

1982 *Still Life in the Age of Rembrandt.* Auckland, New Zealand.

1983 *Landscapes by Rembrandt and His Precursors.* Rembrandthuis, Amsterdam.

1984-1985 *Rembrandt as a Teacher.* Rembrandthuis, Amsterdam.

1986 *Rembrandt: Eaux-fortes.* Musée du Petit-Palais, Paris.

AKNOWLEDGEMENTS

We wish to thank the museums that authorized us to reproduce the works by Rembrandt from their collections.

MUSEEUMS

AUSTRIA: Salzburger Landessammlungen, Residenzgalerie, Salzburg – Kunsthistorisches Museum, Vienna – Kupferstichkabinett, Vienna – Nationalbibliothek, Vienna.

BELGIUM: Musée Royaux des Beaux-Arts, Brussels.

FRANCE: Musée Bonnat, Bayonne – Musée des Beaux-Arts, Lyons – Musée Jacquemart-André, Paris – Musée du Louvre, Paris.

GERMANY: Staatliche Museen, Preußischer Kulturbesitz, Berlin-Dahlem – Wallraf-Richartz Museum, Cologne – Staatliche Kunstsammlungen, Dresden – Städelsches Kunstinstitut, Frankfurt – Kunsthalle, Hamburg – Staatliche Gemäldegalerie, Kassel – Alte Pinakothek, Munich – Staatliche Graphische Sammlung, Munich – Germanisches Nationalmuseum, Nüremberg.

GREAT BRITAIN: National Gallery of Scotland, Edinburgh – Walker Art Gallery, Liverpool – The British Museum, London – National Gallery, London – The Ashmoleum Museum, Oxford.

ITALY: Galleria degli Uffizi, Florence.

NETHERLANDS: Rijksmuseum, Amsterdam – Rijksprintenkabinett, Amsterdam – Teylers Museum, Haarlem – Koninklijke Bibliotheek, The Hague – Mauritshuis, The Hague – Stedelijk Museum de Lakenhal, Leyden – Museum Boymans- van Beuningen, Rotterdam – Stichting Het Catharijenconvent Ruben de Heer, Utrecht.

SWEDEN: Statens Konstmuseer, Stockholm.

UNITED STATES: Museum of Fine Arts, Boston – The Fogg Art Museum, Cambridge, Massachusetts – The Metropolitan Museum of Art, New York.

USSR: Hermitage Museum, Leningrad.

ILLUSTRATIONS

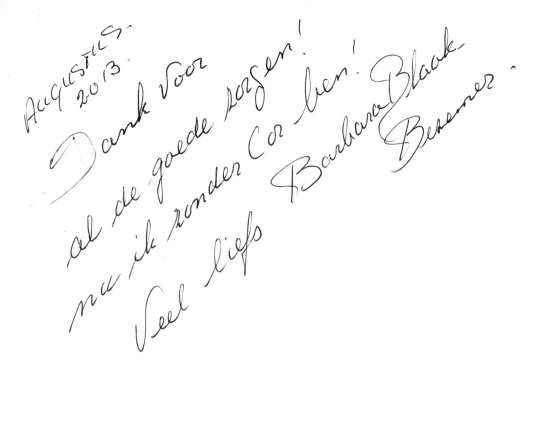

Augustus.
2013.

Dank voor
al de goede zorgen!
nu ik zonder Cor ben!

Veel liefs Barbara Blaak
Bessemer.